Marty's Colour Adventure

a Hutterite colour book

written by
Elma Maendel

illustrated by
Cynthia Stahl

Text © 2010 Elma Maendel
Illustrations © 2010 Cynthia Stahl

Published in Canada by
Hutterian Brethren Book Centre

Box 40 • MacGregor, MB • R0H 0R0 • Canada
P. 204-272-5132 • F. 204-252-2381

All rights reserved.
Reproduction without express written permission in whole or in part,
in any form or medium, of the publisher is prohibited.

The publisher gratefully acknowledges Donna Gamache and
Dora Maendel for their contributions.

Cover design: Yvonne Parks

ISBN 978-0-9865381-2-4

Library and Archives Canada Cataloguing in Publication
A Cataloguing in Publication (CIP) record for this book is available from Library and
Archives Canada.

for my nephew, Jakobi - E. M.

for my children - C. S.

Thanks for rolling along with Marty!

When everyone is hard at work,
The *Kuchl* is my house.
I look for crumbs or cookies,
'Cause I'm hungry Marty Mouse.

Kuchl - Communal Kitchen

This week I'll spend a lot of time
Where tasty food is made.
While Lizzie helps her mom cook meals,
I start my secret raid.

I'll try to learn the colours,
With each food that I devour,
Before Lizzie starts to ring the bell
To tell the mealtime hour.

I see the fridge door left ajar
What treats do I discover?
Cucumbers, lettuce and some peas,
Just perfect for a veggie lover!

I creep down to the floor again
And what do you suppose?
Dear Lizzie slips a carrot stick
Before my eager nose!

Tschierkammela - storage closet for large pots and pans
Tscheinik - teapot

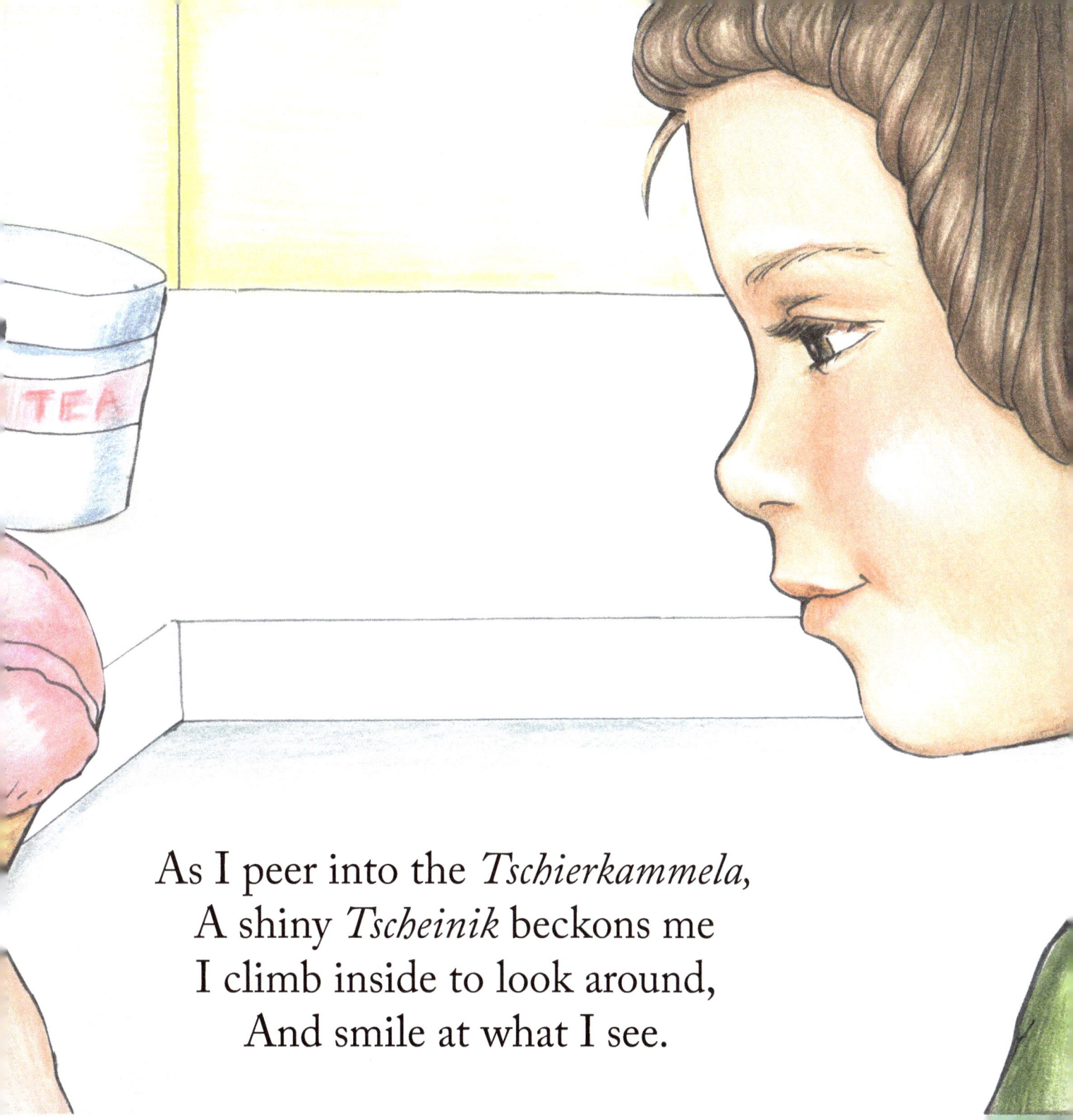

As I peer into the *Tschierkammela*,
A shiny *Tscheinik* beckons me
I climb inside to look around,
And smile at what I see.

Essnschuel - Children's dining room

Scurrying round the corner now,
To the *Essnschuel* I soar
Where Lizzie missed a cob of corn
When she mopped the granite floor.

Next, I make my mousy way
Down to the *Keller* dark
Where I nibble on an eggplant
As big as Noah's ark!

Keller – basement

Down the hall I hurry on
Into the *Kommer*—no time to waste!
Alas, I spill a sack of flour,
But—it's licorice that I taste!

Kommer - Pantry

I slip beneath the *Bochheisl* door
To see what is in store.
A crusty *Zwieboch* waits for me
Below the oven door.

Bochheisl - Bakery
Zwieboch - bun

Before returning to my nest
I yearn for something sweet.
I spy some berries Lizzie dropped—
A lovely juicy treat!

I enjoy each mousy morsel:
Crumbs and tidbits, oh, so sweet!
With your help, I'll learn my colours.
Now, which ones do **you** eat?

Smarties® Cookie

You will need

1 cup margarine
1 ¼ cups brown sugar (lightly pa...
2 eggs
1 teaspoon vanilla
½ teaspoon salt
1 teaspoon baking soda
2 ¼ cups all purpose flour
½ cup Smarties®

Tools needed

Electric mixer, measuring spoons and cups

Marty's Favourite Recipe

What to do

Step 1: Beat margarine and sugar until light and fluffy

Step 2: Add the eggs and mix well

Step 3: Add vanilla, salt, baking soda and flour; mix well

Step 4: Drop by teaspoonful onto cookie sheet, flatten cookies slightly and decorate with Smarties®

Step 5: Bake at 350 °F or 180 °C for 10 to 12 minutes or until they start turning golden brown.

This recipe makes about 30 cookies.

Green

Orange

Pink & Gray

Yellow

Purple

Black & White

Brown

Red & Blue

About the Author

Elma Maendel teaches primary grades at Brennan School on the Elm River Hutterite Community north of Newton, Manitoba, where she has lived all her life. For the past ten years Elma has been a teacher/principal at Brennan School. This is her second adventure with Marty.

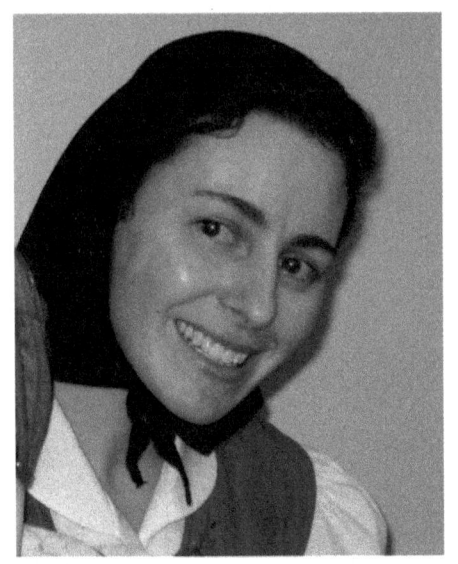

About the Illustrator

Cynthia Kleinsasser Stahl has lived at Odanah Hutterite Community since 2001. She and her husband, Harry, have three children: Renae, Stefan and Darion. Cynthia has worked with children both as a German teacher and an *Essenschuel Mueter*, children's dining room supervisor. Cynthia enjoys art and particularly loves drawing children and animals. Coloured pencils are her main medium.

www.ingramcontent.com/pod-product-compliance
Lightning Source LLC
Chambersburg PA
CBHW061817290426
44110CB00026B/2899